Moving to Panama: Not for Me!

G. Roebuck

Moving to Panama – Not for Me!

Cover Photo: Bridge of the Americas

ISBN-13: 978-1475221091

ISBN-10: 1475221096

CONTENTS

Why This Book was Written

Moving to Panama - Not for me! was written as the definitive guide for those considering moving to Panama to live, work or retire. It covers over 40 topics with worthwhile tips, real-life examples and information. If you are thinking of moving to Panama to retire, or to live in Panama permanently, what you really need to know are the negatives.

This book offers an objective, practical insight into the pros and cons of living in the Republic of Panama. Panama has become a highly rated place for retirement and this book answers the many questions you may have about moving to Panama. It even answers questions you may not have thought of, such as:

- Is Panama safe?
- How much does it cost to buy and run a car?
- Are my favorite foods available – and affordable?
- What is the best visa for me?
- Where will I meet like-minded new friends?
- Do I need vaccinations to visit Panama?
- What should I take to open a bank account?
- What standard of housing is available?
- What is Panama weather like?

The answers will give you food for thought as they take you through day-to-day life in Panama, helping you to make the right decision for yourself personally.

There are many people who are happy to tell you why you should move to Panama – lawyers, realtors and peddlers of retirement dreams, to name a selection. Few if any will tell you the negatives about Panama or Panama City because they do not want to admit, even to themselves, that they have made a mistake. You owe it to yourself to find out the downside of retiring or living in Panama before investing your hard-earned savings in the country.

My personal journey took me to Panama, but for me it clearly became a matter of Living in Panama? No Way! Learn what changed my mind from a commitment to move to Panama to deciding it was definitely not the place for me.

Here's why.

Why I Would Never Retire to Panama

My research for somewhere safe to retire to with high standards of healthcare and a low cost of living, led me to the Republic of Panama. I was guided by my own personal experiences, Internet research and the impressive rating given to Panama by International Living magazine, among other well-respected retirement publications. I was also influenced by informative books written by expats who had recently moved to Panama. Panama certainly seemed to be exactly what I wanted, so, armed with this research, we made our first investigative trip.

We stayed in Panama for three weeks and whittled down our choice of location to Coronado, a friendly community of mainly American and Canadian expats. It is about 55 miles west of Panama City and is a popular area for wealthy Panamanian families and local business owners to have weekend homes. Coronado Panama seemed to tick all the boxes – within easy traveling distance of Tucumen airport and Panama City facilities, on a great beach for walking, enjoying a pleasant year-round climate and having good local amenities.

During our first visit to Panama we set up the initial infrastructure for our return, including opening a bank account, organizing a mail box and searching for suitable rental properties. We planned our next trip to be primarily a buying trip and we booked a casita (small self-catering guest house) to stay in for three months. We greatly looked forward to our return and were highly optimistic that we had a found a place we could live happily into our old age.

However, when we returned to Panama for a longer stay and began to live like locals, we became increasingly aware of some unsettling niggles. Panama real estate is not cheap and certainly not to the standards that westerners are used to. Several people we had met on our previous trip had disturbing stories to tell of burglaries and frightening security issues that had happened during our absence. Some had even put their houses up for sale and were preparing to leave Panama for good.

Buying a second hand car in Panama was a real eye-opener and we began to notice the cost of groceries, electricity and gas were higher than we had realized – in fact considerably higher than in the USA. We also realized that if we were going to make Panama our permanent home, we needed to speak better Spanish.

We became aware that there was an element of corruption among the police force, that emergency services were frankly non-existent and that the already rough roads in Coronado had further deteriorated in the intervening rainy months.

To cut a long story short, we made several more trips to Panama over the next 18 months and finally came to the conclusion that Panama was a great place to visit for a vacation but we would never be totally comfortable living there.

This book was written as an informative resource for those considering moving to Panama, based on our personal experience of what that move would entail. As world travelers with a reasonable amount of street-cred we were never stupid enough to think that Panama was the answer to all our dreams – nowhere is. However, we changed from being determined buyers with a 12-month plan to move to Panama, into deciding that Panama had too many uncomfortable issues for us personally to live there. Sadly the same is true for many more people like us. Some of their eyewitness experiences are recounted in this book, along with true examples of stories to heed.

Moving to Panama: Not for Me!

1. Language in Panama

The official language of Panama is Spanish. However, it is spoken in a distinctly different form than other Spanish speaking countries such as neighboring Colombia and certainly mainland Spain. Dialects and idioms vary throughout Latin American-speaking countries and Panama is no exception.

Although English is widely spoken and understood in Panama City, when it comes down to buying Panama real estate the legal documents are all in Panamanian Spanish. You are at the mercy of an interpreter unless you speak Spanish very well yourself.

True story!

One lady I met who moved to Panama after many years in the USA actually had to attend Spanish lessons to understand and be understood when she moved to Panama. Although she had been born and brought up in Paraguay, the dialect and pronunciation of certain letters was very different. She found herself attending mass in Spanish and not being able to follow it and she also had problems understanding Panamanian legal documents at times.

Most books about moving to Panama emphasize that speaking Spanish is not required, and this is generally true for the spoken word. English is widely spoken in most tourist areas and in Panama City, so you are unlikely to find yourself in an area that has no spoken English. However, as a simple courtesy to your host country and for ease when shopping for groceries, it is easier if you speak some words of Spanish.

Signs, product labeling, legal documents and general information are rarely translated and most restaurants only offer menus in Spanish, so a smattering of the Spanish language is beneficial from the start.

Some waiting staff, shop keepers and supermarket staff do not understand English. You need to be able to make simple requests and say please, thank you and ask for *pensionado* discount in the local language, for your own benefit.

Getting Spanish lessons is very easy – just ask around locally and you will find there is a group class or a bilingual local who will give lessons at a very modest rate per hour.

2. Crime and Security

Panama is listed as one of the safest countries in the Americas and crimes against a person are relatively few. However, home burglaries are very common. If you do not live in a condo with security staff, you must have metal bars on all windows and additional bolts to secure doors. If you want to open the door to allow a breeze in, fit an outer, locking wrought iron gate or door. Panama City tends to have more crime than more rural areas, such as Boquete. Most people use a house sitter or get friends to stay if they are going away for the weekend.

Break-ins are commonplace, even when residents are home asleep. For some reason many homes are targeted within a week of newcomers moving in and on occasions the intruders are armed. Laptops, electrical appliances, gadgets, money, jewelry and valuables tend to be the main items stolen.

Most burglaries tend to be "inside" jobs. Construction workers, plumbers and maids are the first people questioned as suspects by police, so try to use workers who are recommended or can supply references. The disparity between "rich" foreigners and poor locals is often the excuse for staff to justify helping themselves to everything from food and medications to money and jewelry. The best way to avoid security issues is to never leave anything lying around that can be slipped into a pocket or bag.

In Panama City and other main towns in Panama there are frequent ATM robberies, drug-related crimes, kidnapping, occasional shootings and even on one occasion an expat retiree was raped and her husband badly beaten in a home break-in. Take the usual precautions; do not carry large amounts of cash or wear flash jewelry that may make you a target. Be cautious when getting into your vehicle, and always drive in the city with the car windows closed and the doors locked.

The police do follow up reports of crime, but the reality is that if the criminal is not caught in the act, they will never be caught. Unfortunately even those who are caught on serious charges are often released later without punishment. In the past this has led to locals taking the law into their own hands to exact retribution. It may be understandable, but it is not desirable.

True story!

On several occasions we walked down to a deserted beach, put our shirts and shoes in a tidy pile and went down for a swim. We never saw a soul, yet upon our return our clothing and shoes had vanished. We saw builders working nearby on one of the houses and asked them where our shoes were, but they shrugged and said they had not seen anyone. After the first incident we learnt our lesson and instead of wearing our favorite sandals and shirts to go down to the beach, we only took cheap plastic shoes and t-shirts, which also mysteriously vanished.

However, the inconvenience of having to walk back up the burning hot black sands with bare feet is no fun. Likewise, walking along the beach access path which is strewn with sharp stones, broken glass and animal waste was truly distressing. But, as knowing expats continually say with a shrug, “This is Panama”.

3. Police in Panama

The police in Panama are underpaid and are notoriously open to bribes. Motorists in rental cars or driving expensive models are frequently stopped by police for minor offences such as speeding, not being correctly positioned for a turn and other hard-to-define misdemeanors. Expect the policeman to be charming and flattering about yourself and your family before opening his book to point to a recommended fine for the alleged offence. He will then proceed to suggest a lower sum for cash.

One tactic for dealing with the officer is to call his bluff and encourage him to write you a ticket, but the ensuing conversation could be even lengthier than paying the on-the-spot fine. On one such occasion when I was stopped, the police officer finally got down from a suggested fine of $270 to a sum of $20. When the $20 note was handed over, he returned it asking for two $10 notes! Clearly he needed to split the fine with his partner who was sitting waiting in the police car. As yet, this sort of behavior is still part of living in Panama. You will need to decide if and how you will deal with the situation, for it will most certainly arise with annoying regularity when you live anywhere in Panama.

In the case of a burglary or a crime, the police will turn up and seemingly take the matter seriously. In reality, even thieves caught red-handed get off scot-free and any recovered goods do not always find their way back to the original owners.

Although Panama seems very first-world on the surface, these long-standing issues are what still mark it out clearly as a third-world country with high levels of corruption. However, the whole issue has been slightly improved with the recruiting of many women police officers since Martinelli came to power.

4. Emergency Services in Panama

Ambulances appear only to operate in Panama City and if you are not a citizen you are not entitled to their services. You will be expected to take a cab and get yourself to hospital, even if you are bleeding and cannot walk. Unfortunately on two separate occasions known personally to me, expats in a small town had a medical emergency and neither the police nor any ambulance turned up to offer assistance. The outcome in both cases was death, which may or may not have been preventable.

If you decide to live in Panama, you should consider subscribing to a private ambulance service and paying a fixed amount per month for coverage.

True story!

In a large expat community in Panama, concerned residents got together to provide a cell phone for the duty policeman so that in an emergency he could be contacted. The police station telephone seemingly went unanswered.

The residents each paid $1 per month to cover the rental of the cell phone. In return, contributors were given access to the private cell phone number. Although it was an excellent idea and the police seemed keen to embrace it, the idea soon failed as once again the cell phone went unanswered with no reason given. The reality is that Panama does not have the infrastructure and ethics of first world countries, even in the emergency services.

5. Running a Car in Panama

Driving is on the right-hand side of the road and there are a good range of SUVs and cars as in the USA. Pre-owned cars are unbelievably expensive. We were forced to raise our budget to over $3000 to find anything at all. Small runabouts that locals are likely to be able to afford to maintain, such as a Toyota Corona, are extremely pricey for what they are, often with high mileage, a battered exterior and no service history.

You can import a car from the USA to Panama, but be warned, it can be costly. Some expats brought their old but serviceable SUV and on top of shipping costs they had to pay tax to import it. However, the Panamanian customs set the value of the SUV a great deal higher than its US value, making it a very expensive decision that you may want to consider with care. You will certainly need to hire a customs broker who will organize things for you and will arrange the import papers and onward transport to your home.

True story!

In our quest for an old car to use as a runaround for four months, we were surprised to find that there was nothing for sale, even privately, for less than $2500. At that price we were offered an old Toyota sedan with over 200,000 miles on the clock, several battered cars that had obviously been in a number of accidents and even an old taxi that had a smashed windscreen and the passenger door would not open. Buying a car in Panama was a real eye-opener!

Rental cars in Panama are about the same price as in the USA, but that is not practical in the long-term. Buying a new car may be the best solution. Insurance costs are low and include breakdown recovery service, which incidentally is very good.

6. Local Transport

An alternative option to owning your own car is to use local taxis, which is a cheap way to run around the city. Tips are not usually expected. Buses are even cheaper than taxis. Local buses run frequently along the Pan-American Highway, detouring off to local towns along the way. The price for the 55-mile journey from Panama City bus depot at Albrook Mall to Coronado, for example, was just a few dollars. Buses are mostly retired American school buses which are individually painted with cartoon graffiti characters, pictures of the bus driver's wife (and girlfriends!) and perhaps a scene of his home town. Alternatively pick-up minivans are a viable alternative.

Compare the low bus fare with the cost and hassle of driving into Panama City, which involves crossing the congested Bridge of The Americas from the west. However, bus passengers have to endure very loud local music throughout the journey. You may be crammed in with many locals laden with shopping bags, boxes and livestock. On top of that, breakdowns are not uncommon.

7. Utilities in Panama

Most Panama real estate properties that expats will be considering to rent or buy will have electricity, potable drinking water and will be connected to the main sewer. Gas is also available in tanks. There is also both cable and satellite TV and high-speed Internet services within towns and communities.

However, services are far less reliable than in European or American cities. Power will shut off suddenly and unexpectedly, more often than you will be used to. Some modern condos have a generator back-up that kicks in, otherwise you have to sit and wait 2-3 hours for service to be resumed. More frustrating is the fact that water cuts off regularly, even in Panama City. Internet services are only as reliable as the local company, but it is improving.

Electricity is many times more expensive than in the USA and for that reason most homes rely on open doors, fans and breezes to keep cool. The cost of air-conditioning 24/7 would be prohibitive. Generally, running the air-conditioning for an hour before bed and sleeping with a fan is sufficient to stay cool. Some homes have a small media room with a separate air-conditioning unit. This is a good place to store books and paperwork without humidity and offers a cool sanctuary for watching TV without having to cool the whole house.

8. Availability of Communications

Cable and Wireless and Bell South are the two major telephone companies. Pay-as-you-go cell phones are also available.

Internet and TV services can be arranged through a local provider. Expect to put down a deposit before any order to connect is accepted. Local Internet companies are continuing to upgrade the available speeds.

True story!

We paid $120 for a company to install high-speed Internet services before we moved into a rental property. We started to chase the installation the week before our move was due, but on the day of our move the house still had no Internet, but it did have TV. After further phone calls, two installers arrived. They fastened the mast to the roof but there was still no signal, so one of the guys walked across the gardens and shinned nimbly up the tree thought to be blocking the signal. He took his machete and hacked off branches, leaving a horribly disfigured L-shaped tree but still no signal! These cowboys then decided a longer mast was required.

When they left, the Internet was working, but we then discovered the TV was not. They had pulled the TV aerial down and discarded it on the roof, using the taller TV pole to attach their Internet aerial to! We found plenty of cowboys like this in Panama.

9. Furniture and Appliances

There are some local furniture makers in each town and along the side of the road. There are more upmarket furniture shops in Albrook Mall and prices in these stores are roughly equivalent to, or slightly above USA prices, but the quality is good. There is a Do-It-Center chain for smaller household items. For appliances, visit Panafoto at Albrook Mall for a good selection. PriceSmart in Panama City and David also have some appliances, but nothing like the range found in other countries.

In Panama you are best to avoid high-tech appliances as the many power outages throw the complex electrical circuits out of order and they can cost hundreds of dollars to fix. Small electrical appliances are generally not cheap (we bought an electric teakettle for $60 and it lasted less than two weeks). There is unfortunately no guarantee or exchange system for faulty goods in Panama. Electrical appliances tend to be short-lived and poor quality.

A good range of garden furniture such as sun loungers and comfy chairs are harder to find in Panama. They are also much more expensive than in the USA. Consider shipping garden tables, recliners, rockers and cushioned garden chairs from the USA.

True story!

One rental home we stayed in had been newly furnished throughout with local furniture. Apart from being woefully uncomfortable, the furniture did not last long. After a couple of weeks I noticed piles of sawdust beneath each end table and nightstand. Sure enough, telltale holes showed the wood was riddled with termites.

We had to lift all the furniture outside, apart from a few essential pieces, and waited for the owner to treat or replace the items. A few weeks later, I lay in bed one morning when there was a terrible creaking sound. The bed suddenly collapsed with a terrible bang and I ended up on the floor! Further examination showed that the termites had chomped through all the joints of the wooden bed frame and it simply gave way. We spent the rest of that stay sleeping on the floor on a mattress.

10. Staying in Touch with Family Visits

Panama has modern Tocumen International Airport just outside Panama City. It is a major hub for Panama's Copa Airlines, among others, which currently fly to 59 destinations across North, Central and South America and the Caribbean. Copa is also affiliated with Continental/United so options for international flight connections worldwide are good. Generally flights from the USA to Panama are cheap and easy. A second international airport is being built in David to serve West Panama.

True Experience!

Spirit Air has regular flights from Miami and those prepared to fly at unsociable hours can get flights for well under $100. Flights depart Fort Lauderdale at 11.30pm arriving in Panama City 2.20am. The return flight departs 3am from Panama and lands at 5.30am in Fort Lauderdale. However, taxes, compulsory baggage and booking fees can actually more than double those initial flight costs. Those traveling to Panama from further afield will find flights proportionately more expensive.

Although you may not be planning to leave Panama regularly, it is worth considering how easy and affordable it will be for family and friends to visit and stay in touch.

11. Cost of Living in the Republic of Panama

Many books and articles extoll the benefits of retiring to Panama will quote living comfortably on $1200 per month, including rent. I do not have high expectations or an excessive lifestyle, but I found that figure to be ridiculously low and very misleading.

If you own your own home or real estate in Panama, you would save the cost of rental. This would be around $800 per month for a very basic "local" two-bedroom house in a small town such as San Carlos. You can easily pay over $2000 per month for a modern high-rise apartment at Coronado or Playa Blanca, or for a city apartment fitted to American standards.

Running a car will be approximately 10-15% above US costs for gas etc. and food will be slightly higher in price, assuming you buy few imported luxuries and stick to local meat, brands and vegetables. Eating out is slightly cheaper in Panama than the USA.

Electricity will easily run $200 per month, without air-conditioning, plus water and other services. Operating a mailbox will add around $60 per month. Internet services, TV and a phone service all increase your monthly outgoings. Homes up to 20 years old currently are exempt from property taxes, but this may change in the near future. Labor is cheap so a gardener or a maid can cost as little as $15 per day. However, beware of employing staff full time as the labor laws are decidedly not in your favor! You will definitely need a budget for health, whether you choose to pay for a health insurance policy or intend to pay cash for all services and medications as required.

The cost of living in Panama depends upon your own particular standards and what home comforts you consider essential, but you will not live to the standards you may be used to without paying a higher price. See each individual section for more specific information on costs of living, dining out, running a car etc.

12. Groceries

There are several supermarket chains for groceries and other necessities. El Rey and Riba Smith offer a range of American-type products in clean, well-organized stores. Super99 and Machetazo supermarkets tend to be larger and cheaper but do not always have the sort of products or the range that newcomers and expats are looking for.

Local food and vegetables are priced slightly below American prices and local produce such as pineapples are very cheap at around $1 each. Fresh fish and seafood bought at the local fish market or in the supermarket is very affordable. Fresh ground coffee produced in Panama is around $5 per pound. Milk, fresh chicken and meat are slightly above USA prices, but American imports can be shockingly expensive.

Luxury items such as candy, breakfast cereals, tonic water, butter, Philadelphia soft cheese and ice cream can be 50-100% more expensive. Wine is about the same price as in America, and much cheaper than Canada but local beer is very cheap, around 50-60 cents per can.

As a rough guideline, if you are prepared to eat like the locals on cheap cuts of meat, fish, rice and plantains, the cost of living is fairly low. For everything else, be prepared to pay a premium.

13. Shopping in Panama

Most communities have local stores or even a supermarket. Larger towns have a full range of services including banks, vehicle repair shops, hardware stores, drug stores and various other local shops.

In Panama City there are several major shopping malls. Albrook Shopping Mall is behind the central bus depot and has well over 200 shops and stores, a cinema, beauty salons, restaurants and a modern food court, all in air-conditioned comfort. It ranges from local stores such as Panama Hats and El Costo to international brands including Zara, Nautica, Diesel and Perry Ellis.

There are some differences when shopping in Panama, particularly at the Albrook Mall. One significant difference is that security guard outside each store will not let you in with any type of bag, particularly carrier bags of items purchased in other stores. You must deposit your purchases at a small “cubby hole” store where you will receive a receipt for your bags. At the end of your shopping trip, you can return, hand in your receipts and pick up your purchases and bags. Unfortunately this can sometimes involve a very long wait.

There is a larger shopping center at Multicentro Mall at Punta Paitilla attached to the Radisson Decapolis Hotel. Another upmarket experience can be found at the Multiplaza Pacific Mall on Via Israel. It has 280 stores including department stores and many exclusive brands such as Cartier, Louis Vuitton, Guess, Hugo Boss, Jimmy Choo and Swatch.

For those staying along the coast of Panama a new Shopping Village has sprung up on the PanAmerican Highway at the junction with Coronado. It has an excellent range of modern, well-stocked shops including Machetazo, Super 99, Felipe Motta wine store and a host of other shops and services.

Between Panama City and Coronado, the extensive Westland Mall at La Chorrera/Arraijan opened in early 2012 with stores such as Madison, Titan, Conway, Payless Shoes Center, Saks, Crocs, Kenneth Cole, Totto, Arrocha and El Costo. Once completed, this new mall will be one of the largest in Central America.

In all malls be prepared for staff to follow you constantly in department stores – that is their job. Shoplifting is a major problem and shops employ plenty of staff to keep a close eye on all shoppers. You just have to smile and get used to it.

The other problem is that stores (other than international branded chains) do not have a returns policy, even for faulty items. If you buy an electrical appliance and it does not work, you cannot exchange it for another, even with a receipt. Customer service as yet still has to be introduced to Panama.

"We still have two countries — a First World country that's going gangbusters, and a half an hour away, a Fourth World country with too many poor people" - *Roberto Eisenmann, founder of 'La Prensa' newspaper*

14. Working in Panama

If you intend to look for jobs in Panama you must have the correct visa that allows you to do so. Even with that hurdle dealt with, it is very hard to get a job in Panama due to the laws that limit foreign employees. There are specific laws apparently restricting foreign lawyers, doctors, translators and certain other professions from working in Panama.

15. Standards of Dress

You may think that in such a hot country, dress would be very informal, but it is not the case. Even workmen heading to work on a building site will be smartly turned out in a crisply pressed shirt, trousers and polished shoes. After work, they will wash onsite and get dressed smartly to return home.

Panama City is a very well-dressed city. You will never see a local Panamanian wearing shorts or a t-shirt to go shopping or dining out. They will forgive a foreigner for more casual attire, but it is respectful to dress up more than you might back home when you go shopping in the city. You will also find that you are treated with more respect. When in Rome…as they say.

16. Running a Business in Panama

The best way to earn any income is to set up your own business in Panama – but again make sure you have the correct visa and know all the legal requirements before launching forth. If your business involves physical goods and is not selling to the Panama market, you can benefit from operating in the free-trade zone which offers lucrative tax incentives. It is ideal for companies to conduct their business activities in Panama and then ship the goods out without paying any local tax on the profits. This system was set up primarily to encourage import-export businesses to relocate to the area.

If you plan to sell goods to the Panamanian market, corporation tax is 25%. However, if you plan to set up a virtual business, such as an Internet or consultancy business where all your clients are outside Panama, there is no local tax liability, so it is worth considering.

However the territorial tax system in Panama that traditionally provides a popular environment for corporate structure is not favorable for US taxpayers. The IRS considers any standard Panamanian company or "Sociedad Anonima" to be a "per se" corporation and it will therefore always be eligible for US taxes. Owners will find problems such as double taxation and extra tax filings a massive headache as they cannot elect to treat their Panamanian corporation as a pass-through entity. With the additional loss of protection from new banking laws, the advantages of establishing a Panamanian corporation for US taxpayers have all but disappeared compared to the British Virgin Islands, Brunei or the Marshall Islands, where companies still get favorable US tax treatment.

Unlike the US and Europe, the Panama economy is still booming but for expat entrepreneurs the labyrinth of labor restrictions is not business-friendly. For example, the ratio of foreign workers in an authorized business is about 10 locals to one expat. This restricts entrepreneurs from bringing in the best talent from abroad while the local workforce is largely unskilled and transient. Once trained, they are likely to jump ship within a few months to work for someone else.

17. Getting a Visa in Panama

Most first-time visitors to the Republic of Panama will automatically be granted a 90-day tourist visa. You can then apply for an extension for a further 90 days or you must leave the country for at least three days before returning and entering on a new tourist visa. This can be a lot less hassle than trying to obtain an extension from the Immigration authorities.

For those planning to move to Panama permanently, it is essential to begin your application for a permanent visa as quickly as possible. Although the timeline quoted is approximately one year, in reality everything moves painfully slowly with countless delays and it usually takes 2-3 years to complete. In the meantime, having a temporary visa may mean you will have to keep leaving Panama and then returning – a further expense.

You will need a local lawyer, who will charge a four-figure sum for arranging your visa, another cost to add into your calculations. Retiree visas or Pensionado visas are the most popular type of visa for those who are eligible as they have certain benefits. However you are not allowed to work with this visa. Other types of visa to consider are an Investor Visa to run a business, or a Reforestation Visa which is another type of Investor Visa.

Most permanent visas require a police statement from your home country, a health exam and an AIDS test as well as significant investment and a proof of income. After three years you can apply for permanent residency. Your spouse and dependent children will be eligible for a residential visa under your application.

18. Standards of Education in the Republic of Panama

Panama City has three international schools that are fully accredited by the American School Association. In reality, most families moving to Panama need to have their USA educated children put in a higher grade to provide some stimulus and educational challenges.

The International School of Panama (ISP) has the best academic record, and is the only school to offer the International Baccalaureate. It is also the most expensive. The Balboa Academy is more laid back and accommodates children with learning difficulties. The Oxford International School (OIS) is tough if your children do not speak Spanish. The school covers a full American curriculum and a full Panamanian curriculum, which means those in High School will have to study 13 subjects in two languages. The school fees are approximately half of the other schools, but classes are very crowded and there are no after-school programs. The school year at OIS runs from late February through early December.

Some parents opt for home schooling due to the cost and standards of the Panamanian educational system, particularly if their children may later be returned to the American system when they could have fallen well behind in the interim.

19. Republic of Panama Climate

Panama has a humid tropical climate with temperatures between 24-32°C (76-90°F) all year round. It has slightly lower temperatures, less rainfall and less humidity on the Pacific coast than on the Caribbean coast. The higher elevations are cooler, with pleasant afternoon breezes but considerably more rain. The good news is that most days have some sunshine and many immigrants find the climate and humidity are manageable, particularly if you run air-con at night.

The year can be divided into two: the dry season from December through April, and the rainy season from May to November. Thunderstorms are common in Panama but the country is outside the hurricane belt.

True Personal Experience!

During the rainy season Panama is subject to short but heavy torrents of rain, sometimes accompanied by thunder. We were about to drive out of Panama City one afternoon when the heavens opened. It was one of those downpours when the windscreen wipers made no impact whatsoever, with huge drops of rain pelting the glass. We made our way cautiously through the city streets, following the car ahead. The streets were particularly steep and hilly where we were and soon traffic was at a standstill as the floods overwhelmed the drainage system, manhole covers lifted and the roads became fast-flowing rivers.

The water unfortunately collected in dips at the bottom of hills and was soon too deep for cars to drive through. We sat and waited for the shower to pass, knowing it soon would and that the drains would then disperse the floodwaters. We were in a particularly derelict part of town when men suddenly appeared from the empty shops and warehouses wearing loin cloths and nothing else. As the water poured off the roofs onto the sidewalk, they raised their arms and embraced the warm clean water, produced bars of soap and took a free shower!

20. Panamanian Insects

Panama does have several poisonous snakes so care should be taken when walking through grass and undergrowth.

It also has more than its fair share of spiders which can be enormous, highly colorful and in some cases poisonous. Tarantulas are the largest and most intimidating spiders and even a brush with the Tarantula's hairs can cause itching and burning. Scorpion stings are even more prevalent and deadly. Many scorpion species hunt at night, so never walk barefoot outdoors and always shake out your shoes out before putting them on.

At dusk, mosquitoes, sand flies and no-see-ums come out to annoy, bite and buzz. Although windows are screened in modern Panamanian houses, there are no Florida-type pool screens on patios and verandahs. Unfortunately the insects are not just annoying; Panama mosquitos are carriers of malaria, Nile virus, yellow fever and dengue fever. There have been several outbreaks of dengue fever among visitors in recent years and it can be fatal. Use insect repellant containing DEET at all times and try to be indoors at dusk. Alternatively, cover up with long sleeves, pants and shoes.

21. Vaccinations and Disease in Panama

Certain vaccinations are recommended for travelers to Panama over and above the routine vaccinations for influenza, chickenpox, polio, measles, mumps, rubella, diphtheria, pertussis and tetanus. They are:

- Hepatitis A
- Hepatitis B
- Typhoid
- Yellow fever
- Rabies vaccination is recommended for those likely to come into contact with bats, carnivores and other mammals
- Malaria tablets are recommended for those visiting the area to the east of the Panama Canal towards the border of Columbia, where malaria is still prevalent. There are less mosquitos on the Pacific coast

22. Medical Services in Panama

There is no national health service in Panama, as in the UK or Canada. Instead, all medical services including emergency services must be paid for by the recipient. For this reason, health insurance is a must unless you are a gambler or have infinite resources. You can choose a Panamanian policy that only covers major medical emergencies, a policy that also offers international HMOs or one that offers only local HMOs, offering coverage and treatment only in Panama.

The actual cost of seeing a physician or receiving medical treatment in Panama is a fraction of the cost of comparable services in the USA. A visit to the local doctor will be around $5 and although his rooms may be simple, his training and service will be as good as anywhere else. Panamanian hospitals are well equipped with the latest medical equipment and will have doctors and specialists trained in the USA. Consequently most doctors are bilingual and language is rarely a problem.

There are several private hospitals in Panama City including the John Hopkins Hospital in Punta Paitilla, Hospital Nacional, Hospital Santa Fe, Hospital Bella Vista, Hospital Paitilla and San Fernando Clinics in Panama and Coronado. Similar hospitals can be found in David, near Boquete, Panama.

Prescription drugs must be paid for in full but they are generally cheaper than in the USA. Many prescription drugs such as atenolol are available over the counter at pharmacies in Panama. Blood tests, dental treatment and surgery are all very affordable, hence the reason Panama City is a very popular destination for medical tourism. If you are moving to Panama and take out reasonably priced Panamanian health insurance, you should have no problems.

23. Alcohol

Wine, beer and spirits are widely available in supermarkets and restaurants throughout Panama. Local bottled beer is the cheapest drink and even served at a table on the beach it will cost about $1. From the supermarket the cost is closer to 50 cents.

Wine is imported from all over the world and prices are much the same as in America, or possibly a little cheaper. Spirits are also very affordable and most international brands are available. There is a 10% alcohol tax which is added at the checkout. Be aware that on certain national holidays it is prohibited to sell alcohol so you need to plan ahead and stock up.

24. Cultural and Religious Tolerances

There are many differences between native Panamanians and expats besides the language and culture. Churches, traditions and family life all throw up new and different challenges. Panama is a largely Catholic country, as is much of Latin America, but there are also Jewish and other religious faiths represented. Language can be the biggest barrier to worship as most services are conducted in Spanish.

25. Beauty Services

It was a challenge to find trained hair stylists and manicurists in Panama. The best place to start is Albrook Mall in Panama City where at least there is healthy competition. Manicurists will say they can do gel or acrylic nails, but generally they have had no training and will often ask the customer to provide the materials. This shows how infrequently they do the procedure, and that should be a big red flag!

Panamanians tend to want to please and will take the easy way out, promising appointments and services that they have neither the skills not the facilities to complete. Nonetheless they expect to charge US prices for the rather substandard services.

True story!

My wife found a great deal of discrimination against foreigners in smaller beauty salons. She went along to a local salon in one town for a manicure. Despite two girls sitting chatting, she was told there was no availability and to come back the next day at 2pm. She drove home and returned the following day. Again they said they had no-one available and asked her to return later. On the third failed visit, she recognized one of the clients as a local Panamanian neighbor. She explained the situation and asked her to find out what the problem was. Again she elicited a time for my wife to come back the next day - another promise that was not honored.

On another occasion she went to the local beauty shop for a pedicure. It was far from the best pedicure or service, but the cost was $8, so she considered it fair. However, on the next visit she had the same girl and the same treatment. The cost was $28. She asked why the price was so high, but she got no satisfactory reply, of course.

In one beauty shop in Panama she had acrylic nails ripped off and was left with a bleeding nailbed, which took months to heal. On another occasion she requested blond highlights that were so disastrous they had to re-dye her hair back to its original color before she could leave the salon.

If you are moving to Panama, you need to be able to deal with this sort of discrimination and poor treatment and rise above it with a smile. If you can't, you will find, as we did, that life in Panama is wholly frustrating.

"Panama right now is like a beautiful 15-year-old girl who's pretty but doesn't believe she's pretty. She bleaches her dark hair blond to try to get the whole world to like her, but despite herself, her beauty and all her potential are still there" - ***Patrizia Pinzon, Panama City real estate agent.***

26. Managing Local Staff in Panama

Panamanians as a race are gentle and friendly people. They are usually quiet-spoken, unlike some other South American cultures, and are generally easy-going. If you treat them kindly, they will respond with smiles and a helpful attitude. It is never worth losing your temper in Panama as you will certainly not get anywhere, however frustrated you may be. When dealing with staff, make your instructions and requirements clearly known and repeat them as often as is required.

In general you must ask for a task to be done – don't assume that a maid will know that you want things cleaned, so be specific in outlining the day's work. Despite the low wages, staff are entitled to one-month's paid vacation after 11 months and up to 19 bank holidays per year. They are entitled to sick pay and if you fire them, even for blatant theft, they will automatically go to a tribunal and they will win. You must get any employee to sign an employment agreement to control the damage before you hire them as the labor laws in Panama are currently loaded firmly against the employer.

If you are employing a contractor, you need to be very clear about what the job entails, and be firm as to when you expect the job to be completed. Panamanians often have a "manyana" attitude and if you are not insistent they will either not turn up at all or will move on to other jobs where clients are being more insistent.

You should also be prepared to stand over any work to ensure the job is completed correctly, otherwise all sorts of short cuts will be implemented. Be aware that the term "Friday" is always a delaying tactic for sometime the following week. Nothing gets done on Friday in Panama.

You will need to be polite, calm and persistent in order to get even a simple job done. If you lose your temper you will more than likely be “closed off” and nothing will get finished. If you cannot cope with long waits and delays, Panama is probably not the place for you.

It is common to have a housemaid in Panama and most homes have staff to wash dishes, clean floors, do the garden, wash the car, do the laundry and make the beds. However, utilizing local staff does leave you wide open to petty theft, which is rife.

It is hard for locals living in a less privileged existence to see the affluence that foreigners take for granted. It is common for small items, even hair slides, pills, sunglasses, shoes and clothing to disappear without trace. Always secure all valuables, jewelry and money when staff are around or they may prove too much of a temptation.

Unfortunately many break-ins can be traced back to staff providing access, insider knowledge or a duplicate key to accomplices, so be aware of this endemic problem and do not leave yourself open to such problems.

27. Gringo Pricing

It is an accepted fact that as a gringo you will pay more than other residents for the same services. Some people try to use their driver or staff to negotiate on their behalf, but this also backfires. Staff are trained from an early age to stick together against foreigners. As part of the negotiations, your staff will indicate to other parties that they want a cut for your business and so the eventual negotiated price will also include their take. If you do not speak Spanish fluently, consider taping a conversation and getting it translated. The truth is sadly disillusioning – your staff are not on your side.

"Panama is growing like mad and the growing pains are evident in the City where infrastructure is strained to the max, the rich travel in style and the poor line the streets in areas that are still third world" - ***Patrizia Pinzon, local real estate agent and activist with the Casco Viejo Neighborhood Association.***

28. Republic of Panama Banking

In the past, the Republic of Panama has had a reputation for tight banking privacy and any breach of customer details was a punishable offence. However, in 2009 President Martinelli was pressured by the US government to sign one of the most damaging tax treaties in history. The agreement gives the US government complete access to any information regarding Panamanian bank accounts, even without cause. They can mount "fishing expeditions" and Panamanian authorities must comply fully, even when there are no criminal charges. To cover their own backs, Panamanian banks simply closed their doors to US taxpayers, although a few still hold existing personal accounts for Americans, but that window may soon close too. Since it has lost its competitive edge, Panamanian banking has suffered in the international arena.

It is also increasingly difficult for Americans to open bank accounts anywhere in the world due to new United States policies and pressure applied to banks worldwide. You need to be aware of forthcoming capital controls that are likely to be implemented in your home country, which may make it far more difficult and costly to get large sums transferred to Panama. That problem aside, most non-US expats arriving in Panama to open a bank account will need the following:

- Personal reference(s) from your current bank
- Proof of income – certified copies of documents
- Passport
- Cedula – your ID card if you have been accepted for permanent residence
- Two references form Panamanian residents, preferably clients of the bank themselves and in good standing. They may be business associates or friends

- Bank statements for the past six months – some banks also request credit card statements even if you are not applying for a credit card
- Opening deposit in cash – usually a minimum $500 for a checking account and $300 for a savings account.

Opening a bank account in Panama is far more difficult than opening a bank account in your home country. It will take time to follow up references and you should be prepared to chase your application regularly to avoid it stalling completely.

Take note of all the details when you open your bank account in Panama – often steep charges kick in if you do not use the account at least once a year, or if your balance falls below the minimum stated. Rules may change without notice too! Particularly check the fees every month as they may suddenly appear and can quickly drain your balance to zero. Remember that most Panamanian banks do not seem to want your business and make it incredibly slow, difficult and expensive for you to operate an account.

If you need a credit card you will be expected to back it up by investing the equivalent of the credit limit in a separate savings account. Using a preloaded MasterCard may be simpler than jumping through hoops to obtain a credit card and tying up a large balance.

29. Eating Out in Panama

Eating out in Panama is one thing that is definitely cheaper than elsewhere. There are a range of international restaurants offering everything from Peruvian and Italian cuisine to seafood and steakhouses. The best choice and highest standards can be found in Panama City, but elsewhere there are plenty of good options to choose from.

Inevitably there are some restaurants and grills that serve cheap, substandard food but there are plenty of other places to try. Outside Panama City the waiter service is often very unprofessional. Staff would rather watch TV than get up and take your order and if things are not fully cooked or the wrong dish arrives, there is no point in complaining as they have no concept of customer service or how to correct a mistake. Tipping is customary at 10% of the bill.

"From my perspective, the major challenge Panama has is the economic and social polarization," - *Roberto Eisenmann, founder of the Panama City daily newspaper La Prensa.*

30. Mail Services

The Panamanian mail service is not recommended as it is very unreliable. Personal mail delivery to individual homes is unheard of so you will need to organize and pay for a Post Office mailbox. Alternatively, there are two international companies providing mail services in Panama: Air Box Express and Mail Boxes Etc. Both systems operate through a PO Box address in Miami to which all international mail should be addressed. Within that address you have to quote your own mailbox number.

Mail generally takes 2-3 weeks to arrive at your local mailbox center. You then have to line up and sign for your bundle of mail. Some places are woefully disorganized, slow and inefficient. For the privilege of operating a mailbox, you are charged per item for everything you receive, on top of your monthly mailbox rental.

A small bundle of 8-10 letters including junk mail will cost at least \$6. You can also have Amazon orders and magazine subscriptions delivered to your mailbox but they cost even more due to the extra weight and size. This is another consideration to add to your cost of living in Panama. Even if you expect very little mail, it will cost you at least \$60 per month.

For outgoing mail, visit the local *Correos* and make sure you see the stamps are affixed before you leave the counter, for obvious reasons.

31. Social Activities in Panama

Most new arrivals in Panama join one of the expat organizations that are available. "Expats in Panama" hosts a monthly dinner at a local restaurant in Panama City, "Who's New Panama" is a club for women and the "American Society" is also active in Panama City. In Boquete there are monthly meetings for expats and Coronado also has monthly get-togethers and social events.

Socially these groups are relatively small and are not a typical cross-section of society, but at least as expats you all have something in common as a starting point. If you are looking for Red Hats groups, women's clubs, social support groups, Mums and Tots activities and the latest Zoomba keep fit groups you are likely to be disappointed. You may need to consider starting your own club, social group or keep fit club. There are also very few sports bars and no Starbucks for hanging out.

Hobbies are particularly difficult in Panama with no Michael's arts and crafts shops or similar chains offering classes, and few craft materials are available. You may need to order them online, but expect to pay high delivery costs.

32. Sporting Activities and Golf in Panama

Due to the climate, active sports such as tennis generally take place early in the morning or after dark on lighted courts. Fishing, surfing, kayaking, snorkeling, diving and rafting are all available. Swimming pools can be found at Albrook and in most resorts and condominiums. Walking and cycling can be enjoyed along the Amador Causeway. Walking trails can be enjoyed in Omar Torrijos Park, but the best place for walking is on the Pacific beaches where sea breezes offer relative coolness.

Golf can be played at the Santa Maria Golf and Country Club in Costa del Este. The Nicklaus-designed course and park-like surroundings make this a popular but expensive option. The Coronado Golf Club has an 18-hole course designed by Tom Fazio. It is a long-established course which is not particularly well maintained. Golf membership may be grandfathered-in with a home purchase but the annual fee can be very high for the rather substandard amenities.

Most other golf courses are attached to new building projects along the Pacific coast. Joining a golf club in Panama can be very expensive but it may be a good way to integrate and meet new like-minded friends.

33. Shopping in Panama

There is good availability of food, clothing and houseware products throughout Panama. PriceSmart (Costco) is a good source for fresh vegetables and groceries as well as local supermarkets such as Riba Smith, El Rey and the cheaper Super99 and Machetazo supermarkets.

Panama has several shopping malls and markets where clothing and shoes are cheap but American brands, quality and styles are more expensive. Sizing can be a problem with local clothing as Panamanians are generally short and petite. The best option is to buy clothes on a trip to the USA.

34. Currency in the Republic of Panama

What is often cited as an advantage of Panama is the fact that it uses the US dollar. It makes shopping very easy and transferring money without any differing rates of exchange extremely convenient for Americans. However, it means that in the event of a recession in the USA, any income linked to the US dollar will inevitably have massive problems as the cost of imported goods will soar. The dollar has already seen a huge devaluation since the year 2000 and will probably continue to suffer, bringing unnecessary inflationary problems to those living in Panama.

35. Insurances

You will need all the usual types of insurances if you plan to live in Panama. Generally insurance policies are less expensive than elsewhere due to the lack of compensation claims. Car insurance includes the AAA-type recovery insurance which may prove very useful on Panama's rough roads.

Health insurance and private ambulance cover is recommended and can be very reasonable with optional deductibles. If you are buying real estate in Panama you will need title insurance along with optional fire insurance and contents insurance.

Insurance in Panama is generally cheaper than elsewhere and may give peace of mind. However, making a claim can be extremely complicated and you will more than likely have to attend court, even for something as minor as a fender-bender.

36. Political Stability in Panama

Panama is certainly very stable politically. It has no ongoing conflicts with other countries and does not have an active army. While some small countries do not need an army to protect them from enemies, it can sometimes be engaged to control and terrorize its own people. There is nothing like this in peaceful Panama.

Panama has many powerful international allies due to the importance of the Panama Canal. It has a treaty with the United States that will protect the canal if the area is ever threatened and the Chinese have an important self-interest in keeping the canal open for business.

Although there continues to be some corruption in government, Panama has free elections and operates under a democratically elected leader.

"Martinelli's authoritarian administration is running roughshod over the rule of law to attract more foreign investment while ignoring the needs of ordinary Panamanians. At any time we are going to have a social explosion that will be very dangerous" - *Miguel Antonio Bernal, constitutional law professor at the University of Panama*

37. Standard of Living in the Republic of Panama

The Republic of Panama is described as a third world country hiding behind a first-world façade. Certainly Panama City, with its high-rise architecture and modern shopping malls, makes a good first impression. However, beyond the city the true status of the country is more apparent.

You can maintain a good standard of living in Panama as most familiar foods and services are available – at a price. Perhaps most disillusionment with life in Panama is caused by visitors being sold the idea that it is a cheap and modern place to live. Moving to Panama can be very reasonable if you are prepared to live like a local. Other familiar services, foods and a more westernized lifestyle can be found, but they come at a price.

"As shiny Porsches and chrome-tinted Hummers race along the new coastal boulevard, roughly one-third of Panamanians still live in poverty" - *Jason Beaubien, Journalist..*

38. General Healthcare in Panama

Healthcare in Panama is exceptionally high with no real downside. Doctors are often trained in the USA and return to practice their chosen profession in their home country with the added advantage of being bi-lingual.

Equipment is modern, hospitals are clean and well-staffed and costs are comparatively low. Medical tourism in Panama continues to keep its hospitals, dentists and private clinics busy. Those choosing to retire to Panama should consider having some affordable local health insurance as a safety net, should the worst happen.

39. Environment and Infrastructure in Panama

Off the main Pan-American Highway, roads may quickly deteriorate into dirt roads that are not good for your car's suspension and are positively treacherous after heavy rains. Even in the city there may be drains and sewers with missing manhole covers, so walk and drive with extreme care.

You cannot take anything for granted. Footpaths in Panama City may be good in some places and non-existent in others, so take extra care. One unfortunate visitor to Panama City recently stepped on a manhole cover and it immediately pivoted around, plunging her down a dark shaft. Fortunately, her outstretched arms prevented her falling into the fast-flowing effluence but it was a while before she could be pulled out, suffering grazes and shock.

It is an unfortunate generalization but a true one, that most Panamanians do not have any respect for their environment. It is perfectly normal for them to spend a day on a beautiful clean beach and then dump their bottles, litter, carrier bags and dirty diapers on the paths leading down to the beach. Litter is strewn along the roadside in the countryside, from old furniture and tires to black bin bags full of household waste.

True story!

The footpaths giving access to the beach at Coronado run between the beautiful multi-million dollar beachfront houses. However they are unpaved and thick with broken glass, bags of garbage, dog poop and soiled diapers. Thoughtless acts like this make the idea of retiring to Panama seem terribly unattractive, no matter how cheap it may be.

Walking to the beach is like running the gauntlet, holding your nose and hoping for the best. Mango trees overhang the paths and the fruit drops and rots, increasing the stench and attracting bees and insects. There were several public beach access points and all had exactly the same problems to a greater or lesser degree.

40. Standards of Housing in Panama

Buying a lot of land and having a house built can be the cheapest way to get the house of your dreams in Panama at a realistic price. Most of the Panama real estate that meets westernized standards costs at least what the same house would cost in Florida. Luxury condos on the beach start at around $300,000 and luxury villas are closer to $1 million. Away from the coast, prices are slightly lower or you get more land for your money.

Unfortunately many large building projects have failed to materialize or have gone bust and people have lost their deposits. Even if you choose to self-build, it comes with its own challenges and frustrations. Be aware that there are no local building standards or building codes in Panama, so although a house looks OK it may still be hiding a multitude of short cuts and shoddy workmanship.

Even getting an expat to manage the project is not foolproof as many enterprising retirees have set themselves up as contractors or project managers but have no building experience whatsoever. The only successful building project I saw completed, of dozens, was where the couple moved to Panama and spent every moment of the day on site, monitoring the build for many months and inspecting absolutely everything that was done.

The standard of kitchen units, windows and bathroom fitments in Panama is generally not up to American standards and most luxury fittings have to be imported from Europe or the USA.

True story!

I stayed in a newly built house that a Canadian property developer had built as a showhome for gaining future work. That reason alone should have meant it was finished to the best possible standards but it was a series of calamitous and expensive mistakes.

First we arrived almost a month after the house should have been finished. Despite frequent assurances that the house would be completed, furnished and would have Internet connected, we arrived to find the house was still a shell, with no kitchen or bathroom. We had to stay in other accommodation until the house was hastily completed.

When we finally moved in we found:

- The fans were so high and so slow in the vaulted ceiling they were completely ineffective
- The metal roof had no insulation, making the house an oven both night and day
- The air-conditioning units had been installed about 12 feet from the electricity source and had unsightly wires trailing across the walls of the rooms.
- The hot water supply to the shower alternated between cold and scalding hot. For safety we eventually just got used to taking cold showers
- The drain for the shower was situated at the highest point of the shower floor like an island, so the water never drained away
- The interior doors dropped off as the hinges had been put on upside down and the pins gradually worked their way out with gravity
- The tiling was bodged and still covered in grout
- Cupboards were hung unevenly
- Light switches were in the most inconvenient spots possible with no thought or planning

- When it rained, the front verandah floor sloped towards the house and rainwater flooded into the kitchen
- There were gaping holes in the walls, hidden behind furniture, which let in all manner of insects and spiders
- Some air-conditioning units did not work at all

Other unfortunate retirees who had paid to have their dream home built found that:

- The roof leaked seriously and nothing could be done to fix it
- Doors and wooden window frames warped
- Patio doors failed to open and close properly
- Paths cracked and fell away into the garden
- The space for the dishwasher was too small to accommodate an appliance and had to be turned into a cupboard
- Holes in the walls intended for the installation of aircon units had been made too small
- The swimming pool was put in on a slope so it could never be properly filled
- Bats roosted in the attic space causing toxic waste on the bedroom ceiling

Would I have a house built in Panama? Not in a million years!

41. Local Behavior

By and large Panamanians are delightful people – friendly, smiling and rather shy. They are usually willing to help with directions etc. but telling lies and stealing from any easy target is inherent for many. The well-educated business class families often speak good English and we have made some good friends who still welcome us back to Panama and invite us to fundraisers and social events.

As with all societies, some families have obnoxious, spoilt children who tear up and down the public roads and beach on quad bikes (minus mufflers) at all hours of the night, play loud music and are a public nuisance. In the event that youths are caught causing damage or committing misdemeanors, the parents refute all criticism and simply settle the matter by writing a check. Unfortunately discipline of tearaway teenagers is not common in these few minority families and makes living in the neighborhood somewhat stressful.

42. Costs of Buying a Home in Panama

If you intend to buy real estate in Panama, be sure to engage the services of a reputable lawyer, preferably someone who has been recommended to you. Unsuspecting and gullible retirees have on many occasions been swindled out of their life savings, lost their rights to their home or been charged a fortune for relatively straightforward legal services.

Legal rights to land and real estate in Panama are not the same as elsewhere so you need to be sure that you are buying something the seller is legally in a position to sell. Beware of self-financing packages which again may backfire. There are too many sad stories about foreigners being swindled, having trusted a “wonderful Panamanian who had lots of high level connections”. If you do have legal problems, Panama’s legal system is very slow and complicated. Issues will not quickly be resolved, as you would rightly expect in first-world countries.

Another complication is that Panama does not have a central listing service. To see the full range of properties on the market you need to trawl through many agents’ holdings to see what each one has listed for sale.

43. Why the Truth about Moving to Panama is Not Always Told

Many retirees and baby boomers still move to Panama every month and for many it lives up to their expectations. However, many more people discover that Panama is not the place they envisaged. There is sadly a ready supply of homes on the market being sold by expats planning to move out and move on.

Those considering Panama as a place to move to will find plenty of helpful positive "advisors" during their initial research who will tell them what they want to hear. However, buyer beware! Estate agents, lawyers, local shop keepers, restaurateurs and even expats themselves may all have their own reasons for convincing you to move to Panama. For some it is simply a good business move for them – in short they want your business and may be getting a commission or kickback on any home you purchase.

Lonely and unsettled expats may be yearning for new social company or are too proud to admit their mistake. Others cannot afford to sell up and move elsewhere and are making the best of a bad decision. They are unlikely to tell you why you should not move to Panama.

If you are considering moving to Panama, as well as buying magazines and books that tell you all the plus points about this Central American country (perhaps with rather rose-tinted spectacles), you need a truthful guide to point out why you should perhaps NOT move to Panama.

This book has pinpointed over 40 important issues about living in Panama and covers the good and bad points of each. It aims to tell you the truth, as we saw it, about what you *really* need to know so you can make an informed decision about your life-changing move to Panama.

Panama is not for everyone and some people regret their decision to move there as it simply does not live up to their expectations. The frustrations of living in a developing country, the inefficiency, dishonesty and disorganization may all prove to be too much and some visitors simply become frustrated, depressed and eventually leave.

Panama does seem to attract an unusually high number of "characters". I met several people who admitted they were running away from something – money, health problems, bad relationships, family issues, legal, tax or business problems. For some, the chance to start over is eagerly seized, but for others moving to Panama adds yet more problems. Homesickness, the humid climate and being unable to adapt are three key issues to consider. Many expats have arrived in Panama with entrepreneurial vision, but doing business as a foreigner is very tough and the failure rate for businesses can be high.

You may disregard these points as unimportant to you, but if you don't know the negatives of moving to Panama, can you really make an informed choice? Before you invest your hopes, life-savings, aspirations, health and future social life in the Republic of Panama, you need to understand the full picture. You will then be better positioned to decide for yourself whether moving to Panama is the right choice for you.

Made in the USA
Lexington, KY
25 September 2013